. . . .

this book belongs to

Created & Designed By Valerie Aiello

ISBN: 978-0-9913388-7-0 (Hardcover)

Published By Goal Party

Austin, Texas

United States of America

www.goalparty.com

personal
brand diary

Personal Brand Diary is a guided journal that keeps your big picture business components and thoughts chronicled, archived, and organized in one place.

Write in the prompted journal pages for a two-page overview of how you can strategize and implement your personal brand ideas. Date and fill out pages as often as you would like. Use the following blank pages to write, doodle, brainstorm, collage, mindmap, visualize, daydream, think, draw or simply journal whatever is on your mind. Expand on your innovation and strategies in the medium style that works for you.

Complete each set of four pages. Return to previous dates to review goals you are still working towards, goals you have achieved, or goals simply forgotten. Then, start again when you have time to sit and organize inside your *Personal Brand Diary.*

mission statement

daily goals

weekly goals

three month goals

one year goals

five year goals

ten year goals

JOURNAL

how's it going?

physically

intellectually

financially

socially

professionally

spiritually

relaxation levels

living space

LIST
expert skills

- ○
- ○
- ○
- ○
- ○

LIST
unique qualities

- ○
- ○
- ○
- ○
- ○

LIST
brand value to customers

- ○
- ○
- ○
- ○
- ○

LIST
achievements

- ○
- ○
- ○
- ○
- ○

LIST
vulnerabilities

- ○
- ○
- ○
- ○
- ○

revenue streams	problem solved	value created

operating expenses	sales goals	profits
●	●	●
●	●	●
●	●	●
●	●	●
●	●	●
total	total	total

CHECKLIST
customer communication

PRESS RELEASE
outlets press release sent to:

- website
- email
- text
- phone call
- direct messages

LIST
how people describe me
- ●
- ●
- ●
- ●
- ●

LIST
customer opinions
- ●
- ●
- ●
- ●
- ●

LIST
events for customers
- ●
- ●
- ●
- ●
- ●

LIST
things to learn
- ●
- ●
- ●
- ●
- ●

LIST
inspirational brands
- ●
- ●
- ●
- ●
- ●

LIST
favorite books & shows
- ●
- ●
- ●
- ●
- ●

JOURNAL
how customers discover brand

AUDIO: **brand podcast**

VISUAL: **brand shows & live streams**

WRITE ARTICLES: **online & print media**

PRESS: **publicity plan & interviews**

COLLABORATIONS: **brands & influencers**

ADVERTISING: **types & placements**

MARKETING: **digital collateral**

MARKETING: **traditional collateral**

mission statement

daily goals

weekly goals

three month goals

one year goals

five year goals

ten year goals

JOURNAL

how's it going?

physically

intellectually

financially

socially

professionally

spiritually

relaxation levels

living space

LIST
expert skills

-
-
-
-
-

LIST
unique qualities

-
-
-
-
-

LIST
brand value to customers

-
-
-
-
-

LIST
achievements

-
-
-
-
-

LIST
vulnerabilities

-
-
-
-
-

revenue streams	problem solved	value created

operating expenses	sales goals	profits
○	○	○
○	○	○
○	○	○
○	○	○
○	○	○
total	total	total

CHECKLIST
customer communication

- website
- email
- text
- phone call
- direct messages

PRESS RELEASE
outlets press release sent to:

LIST
how people describe me
- ○
- ○
- ○
- ○
- ○

LIST
customer opinions
- ○
- ○
- ○
- ○
- ○

LIST
events for customers
- ○
- ○
- ○
- ○
- ○

LIST
things to learn
- ○
- ○
- ○
- ○
- ○

LIST
inspirational brands
- ○
- ○
- ○
- ○
- ○

LIST
favorite books & shows
- ○
- ○
- ○
- ○
- ○

JOURNAL
how customers discover brand

AUDIO: brand podcast

VISUAL: brand shows & live streams

WRITE ARTICLES: online & print media

PRESS: publicity plan & interviews

COLLABORATIONS: brands & influencers

ADVERTISING: types & placements

MARKETING: digital collateral

MARKETING: traditional collateral

mission statement

daily goals

weekly goals

three month goals

one year goals

five year goals

ten year goals

date _____

JOURNAL

how's it going?

physically

intellectually

financially

socially

professionally

spiritually

relaxation levels

living space

LIST
expert skills

LIST
unique qualities

LIST
brand value to customers

LIST
achievements

LIST
vulnerabilities

revenue streams	problem solved	value created

operating expenses	sales goals	profits
○	○	○
○	○	○
○	○	○
○	○	○
○	○	○
total	total	total

CHECKLIST
customer communication

- website
- email
- text
- phone call
- direct messages

PRESS RELEASE
outlets press release sent to:

LIST
how people describe me

○
○
○
○
○

LIST
customer opinions

○
○
○
○
○

LIST
events for customers

○
○
○
○
○

LIST
things to learn

○
○
○
○
○

LIST
inspirational brands

○
○
○
○
○

LIST
favorite books & shows

○
○
○
○
○

JOURNAL
how customers discover brand

AUDIO: brand podcast

VISUAL: brand shows & live streams

WRITE ARTICLES: online & print media

PRESS: publicity plan & interviews

COLLABORATIONS: brands & influencers

ADVERTISING: types & placements

MARKETING: digital collateral

MARKETING: traditional collateral

mission statement

daily goals

weekly goals

three month goals

one year goals

five year goals

ten year goals

JOURNAL

how's it going?

physically

intellectually

financially

socially

professionally

spiritually

relaxation levels

living space?

LIST
expert skills

*
*
*
*
*

LIST
unique qualities

*
*
*
*
*

LIST
brand value to customers

*
*
*
*
*

LIST
achievements

*
*
*
*
*

LIST
vulnerabilities

*
*
*
*
*

revenue streams	problem solved	value created

operating expenses	sales goals	profits
●	●	●
●	●	●
●	●	●
●	●	●
●	●	●
total	total	total

CHECKLIST
customer communication

- website
- email
- text
- phone call
- direct messages
-

PRESS RELEASE
outlets press release sent to:

LIST
how people describe me

- ●
- ●
- ●
- ●
- ●

LIST
customer opinions

- ●
- ●
- ●
- ●
- ●

LIST
events for customers

- ●
- ●
- ●
- ●
- ●

LIST
things to learn

- ●
- ●
- ●
- ●
- ●

LIST
inspirational brands

- ●
- ●
- ●
- ●
- ●

LIST
favorite books & shows

- ●
- ●
- ●
- ●
- ●

JOURNAL
how customers discover brand

AUDIO: brand podcast

VISUAL: brand shows & live streams

WRITE ARTICLES: online & print media

PRESS: publicity plan & interviews

COLLABORATIONS: brands & influencers

ADVERTISING: types & placements

MARKETING: digital collateral

MARKETING: traditional collateral

mission statement

daily goals

weekly goals

three month goals

one year goals

five year goals

ten year goals

JOURNAL

how's it going?

physically

intellectually

financially

socially

professionally

spiritually

relaxation levels

living space

LIST
expert skills

- ⊛
- ⊛
- ⊛
- ⊛
- ⊛

LIST
unique qualities

- ⊛
- ⊛
- ⊛
- ⊛
- ⊛

LIST
brand value to customers

- ⊛
- ⊛
- ⊛
- ⊛
- ⊛

LIST
achievements

- ⊛
- ⊛
- ⊛
- ⊛
- ⊛

LIST
vulnerabilities

- ⊛
- ⊛
- ⊛
- ⊛
- ⊛

revenue streams	problem solved	value created

operating expenses	sales goals	profits
⊙	⊙	⊙
⊙	⊙	⊙
⊙	⊙	⊙
⊙	⊙	⊙
⊙	⊙	⊙
total	total	total

CHECKLIST
customer communication

- [ ] website
- [ ] email
- [ ] text
- [ ] phone call
- [ ] direct messages
- [ ]

PRESS RELEASE
outlets press release sent to:

LIST
how people describe me
- ⊙
- ⊙
- ⊙
- ⊙
- ⊙

LIST
customer opinions
- ⊙
- ⊙
- ⊙
- ⊙
- ⊙

LIST
events for customers
- ⊙
- ⊙
- ⊙
- ⊙
- ⊙

LIST
things to learn
- ⊙
- ⊙
- ⊙
- ⊙
- ⊙

LIST
inspirational brands
- ⊙
- ⊙
- ⊙
- ⊙
- ⊙

LIST
favorite books & shows
- ⊙
- ⊙
- ⊙
- ⊙
- ⊙

JOURNAL
how customers discover brand

AUDIO: brand podcast

VISUAL: brand shows & live streams

WRITE ARTICLES: online & print media

PRESS: publicity plan & interviews

COLLABORATIONS: brands & influencers

ADVERTISING: types & placements

MARKETING: digital collateral

MARKETING: traditional collateral

mission statement

daily goals

weekly goals

three month goals

one year goals

five year goals

ten year goals

JOURNAL

how's it going?

physically

intellectually

financially

socially

professionally

spiritually

relaxation levels

living space

LIST
expert skills

-
-
-
-
-

LIST
unique qualities

-
-
-
-
-

LIST
brand value to customers

-
-
-
-
-

LIST
achievements

-
-
-
-
-

LIST
vulnerabilities

-
-
-
-

revenue streams	problem solved	value created

operating expenses	sales goals	profits
○	○	○
○	○	○
○	○	○
○	○	○
○	○	○
total	total	total

CHECKLIST
customer communication

- [ ] website
- [ ] email
- [ ] text
- [ ] phone call
- [ ] direct messages
- [ ]

PRESS RELEASE
outlets press release sent to:

LIST
how people describe me
- ○
- ○
- ○
- ○
- ○

LIST
customer opinions
- ○
- ○
- ○
- ○
- ○

LIST
events for customers
- ○
- ○
- ○
- ○
- ○

LIST
things to learn
- ○
- ○
- ○
- ○
- ○

LIST
inspirational brands
- ○
- ○
- ○
- ○
- ○

LIST
favorite books & shows
- ○
- ○
- ○
- ○
- ○

JOURNAL
how customers discover brand

AUDIO: brand podcast

VISUAL: brand shows & live streams

WRITE ARTICLES: online & print media

PRESS: publicity plan & interviews

COLLABORATIONS: brands & influencers

ADVERTISING: types & placements

MARKETING: digital collateral

MARKETING: traditional collateral

mission statement

daily goals

weekly goals

three month goals

one year goals

five year goals

ten year goals

JOURNAL
how's it going?

physically

intellectually

financially

socially

professionally

spiritually

relaxation levels

living space

LIST
expert skills

LIST
unique qualities

LIST
brand value to customers

LIST
achievements

LIST
vulnerabilities

revenue streams	problem solved	value created

operating expenses	sales goals	profits
◦	◦	◦
◦	◦	◦
◦	◦	◦
◦	◦	◦
◦	◦	◦
total	total	total

AUDIO: brand podcast

VISUAL: brand shows & live streams

WRITE ARTICLES: online & print media

CHECKLIST
customer communication

- website
- email
- text
- phone call
- direct messages

PRESS RELEASE
outlets press release sent to:

PRESS: publicity plan & interviews

COLLABORATIONS: brands & influencers

LIST
how people describe me
- ◦
- ◦
- ◦
- ◦
- ◦

LIST
customer opinions
- ◦
- ◦
- ◦
- ◦
- ◦

LIST
events for customers
- ◦
- ◦
- ◦
- ◦
- ◦

ADVERTISING: types & placements

LIST
things to learn
- ◦
- ◦
- ◦
- ◦
- ◦

LIST
inspirational brands
- ◦
- ◦
- ◦
- ◦
- ◦

LIST
favorite books & shows
- ◦
- ◦
- ◦
- ◦
- ◦

MARKETING: digital collateral

MARKETING: traditional collateral

mission statement

daily goals

weekly goals

three month goals

one year goals

five year goals

ten year goals

mission statement

date _____

how's it going?

physically

intellectually

financially

socially

professionally

spiritually

relaxation levels

living space

expert skills

⊛
⊛
⊛
⊛
⊛

unique qualities

⊛
⊛
⊛
⊛
⊛

brand value to customers

⊛
⊛
⊛
⊛
⊛

achievements

⊛
⊛
⊛
⊛
⊛

vulnerabilities

⊛
⊛
⊛
⊛

revenue streams	problem solved	value created

operating expenses	sales goals	profits
○	○	○
○	○	○
○	○	○
○	○	○
○	○	○
total	total	total

CHECKLIST
customer communication

- website
- email
- text
- phone call
- direct messages

PRESS RELEASE
outlets press release sent to:

LIST
how people describe me
- ○
- ○
- ○
- ○
- ○

LIST
customer opinions
- ○
- ○
- ○
- ○
- ○

LIST
events for customers
- ○
- ○
- ○
- ○
- ○

LIST
things to learn
- ○
- ○
- ○
- ○
- ○

LIST
inspirational brands
- ○
- ○
- ○
- ○
- ○

LIST
favorite books & shows
- ○
- ○
- ○
- ○
- ○

JOURNAL
how customers discover brand

AUDIO: **brand podcast**

VISUAL: **brand shows & live streams**

WRITE ARTICLES: **online & print media**

PRESS: **publicity plan & interviews**

COLLABORATIONS: **brands & influencers**

ADVERTISING: **types & placements**

MARKETING: **digital collateral**

MARKETING: **traditional collateral**

mission statement

daily goals

weekly goals

three month goals

one year goals

five year goals

ten year goals

JOURNAL

how's it going?

physically

intellectually

financially

socially

professionally

spiritually

relaxation levels

living space

LIST
expert skills

⊛
⊛
⊛
⊛
⊛

LIST
unique qualities

⊛
⊛
⊛
⊛
⊛

LIST
brand value to customers

⊛
⊛
⊛
⊛
⊛

LIST
achievements

⊛
⊛
⊛
⊛
⊛

LIST
vulnerabilities

⊛
⊛
⊛
⊛
⊛

revenue streams	problem solved	value created

operating expenses	sales goals	profits
◌	◌	◌
◌	◌	◌
◌	◌	◌
◌	◌	◌
◌	◌	◌
total	total	total

CHECKLIST
customer communication

- [ ] website
- [ ] email
- [ ] text
- [ ] phone call
- [ ] direct messages
- [ ]

PRESS RELEASE
outlets press release sent to:

LIST
how people describe me
- ◌
- ◌
- ◌
- ◌
- ◌

LIST
customer opinions
- ◌
- ◌
- ◌
- ◌
- ◌

LIST
events for customers
- ◌
- ◌
- ◌
- ◌
- ◌

LIST
things to learn
- ◌
- ◌
- ◌
- ◌
- ◌

LIST
inspirational brands
- ◌
- ◌
- ◌
- ◌
- ◌

LIST
favorite books & shows
- ◌
- ◌
- ◌
- ◌
- ◌

JOURNAL
how customers discover brand

AUDIO: **brand podcast**

VISUAL: **brand shows & live streams**

WRITE ARTICLES: **online & print media**

PRESS: **publicity plan & interviews**

COLLABORATIONS: **brands & influencers**

ADVERTISING: **types & placements**

MARKETING: **digital collateral**

MARKETING: **traditional collateral**

mission statement

daily goals

weekly goals

three month goals

one year goals

five year goals

ten year goals

JOURNAL

how's it going?

physically

intellectually

financially

socially

professionally

spiritually

relaxation levels

living space

LIST
expert skills

  ●
  ●
  ●
  ●
  ●

LIST
unique qualities

  ●
  ●
  ●
  ●
  ●

LIST
brand value to customers

  ●
  ●
  ●
  ●
  ●

LIST
achievements

  ●
  ●
  ●
  ●
  ●

LIST
vulnerabilities

  ●
  ●
  ●
  ●

revenue streams	problem solved	value created

how customers discover brand

operating expenses	sales goals	profits
○	○	○
○	○	○
○	○	○
○	○	○
○	○	○
total	total	total

AUDIO: brand podcast

VISUAL: brand shows & live streams

WRITE ARTICLES: online & print media

CHECKLIST
customer communication

PRESS RELEASE
outlets press release sent to:

- website
- email
- text
- phone call
- direct messages

PRESS: publicity plan & interviews

COLLABORATIONS: brands & influencers

LIST
how people describe me
- ○
- ○
- ○
- ○
- ○

LIST
customer opinions
- ○
- ○
- ○
- ○
- ○

LIST
events for customers
- ○
- ○
- ○
- ○
- ○

ADVERTISING: types & placements

LIST
things to learn
- ○
- ○
- ○
- ○
- ○

LIST
inspirational brands
- ○
- ○
- ○
- ○
- ○

LIST
favorite books & shows
- ○
- ○
- ○
- ○
- ○

MARKETING: digital collateral

MARKETING: traditional collateral

mission statement

daily goals

weekly goals

three month goals

one year goals

five year goals

ten year goals

JOURNAL

how's it going?

physically

intellectually

financially

socially

professionally

spiritually

relaxation levels

living space

LIST
expert skills

-
-
-
-
-

LIST
unique qualities

-
-
-
-
-

LIST
brand value to customers

-
-
-
-
-

LIST
achievements

-
-
-
-
-

LIST
vulnerabilities

-
-
-
-

revenue streams	problem solved	value created

operating expenses	sales goals	profits
●	●	●
●	●	●
●	●	●
●	●	●
●	●	●
total	total	total

CHECKLIST
customer communication

- [ ] website
- [ ] email
- [ ] text
- [ ] phone call
- [ ] direct messages
- [ ]

PRESS RELEASE
outlets press release sent to:

LIST
how people describe me
- ●
- ●
- ●
- ●
- ●

LIST
customer opinions
- ●
- ●
- ●
- ●
- ●

LIST
events for customers
- ●
- ●
- ●
- ●
- ●

LIST
things to learn
- ●
- ●
- ●
- ●
- ●

LIST
inspirational brands
- ●
- ●
- ●
- ●
- ●

LIST
favorite books & shows
- ●
- ●
- ●
- ●
- ●

JOURNAL
how customers discover brand

AUDIO: brand podcast

VISUAL: brand shows & live streams

WRITE ARTICLES: online & print media

PRESS: publicity plan & interviews

COLLABORATIONS: brands & influencers

ADVERTISING: types & placements

MARKETING: digital collateral

MARKETING: traditional collateral

mission statement

daily goals

weekly goals

three month goals

one year goals

five year goals

ten year goals

JOURNAL
how's it going?

physically

intellectually

financially

socially

professionally

spiritually

relaxation levels

living space

LIST
expert skills

- ⚙
- ⚙
- ⚙
- ⚙
- ⚙

LIST
unique qualities

- ⚙
- ⚙
- ⚙
- ⚙
- ⚙

LIST
brand value to customers

- ⚙
- ⚙
- ⚙
- ⚙
- ⚙

LIST
achievements

- ⚙
- ⚙
- ⚙
- ⚙
- ⚙

LIST
vulnerabilities

- ⚙
- ⚙
- ⚙
- ⚙

revenue streams	problem solved	value created

JOURNAL
how customers discover brand

AUDIO: brand podcast

operating expenses	sales goals	profits
●	●	●
●	●	●
●	●	●
●	●	●
●	●	●
total	total	total

VISUAL: brand shows & live streams

WRITE ARTICLES: online & print media

CHECKLIST
customer communication

PRESS RELEASE
outlets press release sent to:

- website
- email
- text
- phone call
- direct messages

PRESS: publicity plan & interviews

COLLABORATIONS: brands & influencers

LIST
how people describe me

LIST
customer opinions

LIST
events for customers

- ●
- ●
- ●
- ●
- ●

ADVERTISING: types & placements

LIST
things to learn

LIST
inspirational brands

LIST
favorite books & shows

MARKETING: digital collateral

MARKETING: traditional collateral

mission statement

daily goals

weekly goals

three month goals

one year goals

five year goals

ten year goals

JOURNAL

how's it going?

physically

intellectually

financially

socially

professionally

spiritually

relaxation levels

living space

LIST
expert skills

LIST
unique qualities

LIST
brand value to customers

LIST
achievements

LIST
vulnerabilities

revenue streams	problem solved	value created

operating expenses	sales goals	profits
◦	◦	◦
◦	◦	◦
◦	◦	◦
◦	◦	◦
◦	◦	◦
total	total	total

CHECKLIST
customer communication

☐ website

☐ email

☐ text

☐ phone call

☐ direct messages

☐

PRESS RELEASE
outlets press release sent to:

LIST
how people describe me

◦

◦

◦

◦

◦

LIST
customer opinions

◦

◦

◦

◦

◦

LIST
events for customers

◦

◦

◦

◦

◦

LIST
things to learn

◦

◦

◦

◦

◦

LIST
inspirational brands

◦

◦

◦

◦

◦

LIST
favorite books & shows

◦

◦

◦

◦

◦

JOURNAL
how customers discover brand

AUDIO: **brand podcast**

VISUAL: **brand shows & live streams**

WRITE ARTICLES: **online & print media**

PRESS: **publicity plan & interviews**

COLLABORATIONS: **brands & influencers**

ADVERTISING: **types & placements**

MARKETING: **digital collateral**

MARKETING: **traditional collateral**

mission statement

daily goals

weekly goals

three month goals

one year goals

five year goals

ten year goals

JOURNAL

how's it going?

physically

intellectually

financially

socially

professionally

spiritually

relaxation levels

living space

LIST
expert skills

LIST
unique qualities

LIST
brand value to customers

LIST
achievements

LIST
vulnerabilities

revenue streams	problem solved	value created

operating expenses	sales goals	profits
○	○	○
○	○	○
○	○	○
○	○	○
○	○	○
total	total	total

CHECKLIST
customer communication

- [ ] website
- [ ] email
- [ ] text
- [ ] phone call
- [ ] direct messages
- [ ] _____

PRESS RELEASE
outlets press release sent to:

LIST
how people describe me

- ○
- ○
- ○
- ○
- ○

LIST
customer opinions

- ○
- ○
- ○
- ○
- ○

LIST
events for customers

- ○
- ○
- ○
- ○
- ○

LIST
things to learn

- ○
- ○
- ○
- ○
- ○

LIST
inspirational brands

- ○
- ○
- ○
- ○
- ○

LIST
favorite books & shows

- ○
- ○
- ○
- ○
- ○

JOURNAL
how customers discover brand

AUDIO: brand podcast

VISUAL: brand shows & live streams

WRITE ARTICLES: online & print media

PRESS: publicity plan & interviews

COLLABORATIONS: brands & influencers

ADVERTISING: types & placements

MARKETING: digital collateral

MARKETING: traditional collateral

mission statement

daily goals

weekly goals

three month goals

one year goals

five year goals

ten year goals

JOURNAL

how's it going?

physically

intellectually

financially

socially

professionally

spiritually

relaxation levels

living space

LIST
expert skills

- ○
- ○
- ○
- ○
- ○

LIST
unique qualities

- ○
- ○
- ○
- ○
- ○

LIST
brand value to customers

- ○
- ○
- ○
- ○
- ○

LIST
achievements

- ○
- ○
- ○
- ○
- ○

LIST
vulnerabilities

- ○
- ○
- ○
- ○
- ○

revenue streams	problem solved	value created

operating expenses	sales goals	profits
○	○	○
○	○	○
○	○	○
○	○	○
○	○	○
total	total	total

CHECKLIST
customer communication

- website
- email
- text
- phone call
- direct messages
- _____

PRESS RELEASE
outlets press release sent to:

LIST
how people describe me
- ○
- ○
- ○
- ○
- ○

LIST
customer opinions
- ○
- ○
- ○
- ○
- ○

LIST
events for customers
- ○
- ○
- ○
- ○
- ○

LIST
things to learn
- ○
- ○
- ○
- ○
- ○

LIST
inspirational brands
- ○
- ○
- ○
- ○
- ○

LIST
favorite books & shows
- ○
- ○
- ○
- ○
- ○

JOURNAL
how customers discover brand

AUDIO: brand podcast

VISUAL: brand shows & live streams

WRITE ARTICLES: online & print media

PRESS: publicity plan & interviews

COLLABORATIONS: brands & influencers

ADVERTISING: types & placements

MARKETING: digital collateral

MARKETING: traditional collateral

mission statement

daily goals

weekly goals

three month goals

one year goals

five year goals

ten year goals

JOURNAL
how's it going?

physically

intellectually

financially

socially

professionally

spiritually

relaxation levels

living space

LIST
expert skills

LIST
unique qualities

LIST
brand value to customers

LIST
achievements

LIST
vulnerabilities

revenue streams	problem solved	value created

operating expenses	sales goals	profits
○	○	○
○	○	○
○	○	○
○	○	○
○	○	○
total	total	total

CHECKLIST
customer communication

- website
- email
- text
- phone call
- direct messages
-

PRESS RELEASE
outlets press release sent to:

LIST
how people describe me

- ○
- ○
- ○
- ○
- ○

LIST
customer opinions

- ○
- ○
- ○
- ○
- ○

LIST
events for customers

- ○
- ○
- ○
- ○
- ○

LIST
things to learn

- ○
- ○
- ○
- ○
- ○

LIST
inspirational brands

- ○
- ○
- ○
- ○
- ○

LIST
favorite books & shows

- ○
- ○
- ○
- ○
- ○

JOURNAL
how customers discover brand

AUDIO: brand podcast

VISUAL: brand shows & live streams

WRITE ARTICLES: online & print media

PRESS: publicity plan & interviews

COLLABORATIONS: brands & influencers

ADVERTISING: types & placements

MARKETING: digital collateral

MARKETING: traditional collateral

mission statement

daily goals

weekly goals

three month goals

one year goals

five year goals

ten year goals

JOURNAL

how's it going?

physically

intellectually

financially

socially

professionally

spiritually

relaxation levels

living space

LIST
expert skills

- ●
- ●
- ●
- ●
- ●

LIST
unique qualities

- ●
- ●
- ●
- ●
- ●

LIST
brand value to customers

- ●
- ●
- ●
- ●
- ●

LIST
achievements

- ●
- ●
- ●
- ●
- ●

LIST
vulnerabilities

- ●
- ●
- ●
- ●
- ●

revenue streams	problem solved	value created

JOURNAL

how customers discover brand

operating expenses	sales goals	profits
○	○	○
○	○	○
○	○	○
○	○	○
○	○	○
total	total	total

AUDIO: brand podcast

VISUAL: brand shows & live streams

CHECKLIST
customer communication

- website
- email
- text
- phone call
- direct messages
- ___

PRESS RELEASE
outlets press release sent to:

WRITE ARTICLES: online & print media

PRESS: publicity plan & interviews

COLLABORATIONS: brands & influencers

LIST
how people describe me

- ○
- ○
- ○
- ○
- ○

LIST
customer opinions

- ○
- ○
- ○
- ○
- ○

LIST
events for customers

- ○
- ○
- ○
- ○
- ○

ADVERTISING: types & placements

LIST
things to learn

- ○
- ○
- ○
- ○
- ○

LIST
inspirational brands

- ○
- ○
- ○
- ○
- ○

LIST
favorite books & shows

- ○
- ○
- ○
- ○
- ○

MARKETING: digital collateral

MARKETING: traditional collateral

mission statement

daily goals

weekly goals

three month goals

one year goals

five year goals

ten year goals

JOURNAL

how's it going?

physically

intellectually

financially

socially

professionally

spiritually

relaxation levels

living space

LIST
expert skills

⚬
⚬
⚬
⚬
⚬

LIST
unique qualities

⚬
⚬
⚬
⚬
⚬

LIST
brand value to customers

⚬
⚬
⚬
⚬
⚬

LIST
achievements

⚬
⚬
⚬
⚬
⚬

LIST
vulnerabilities

⚬
⚬
⚬
⚬
⚬

revenue streams	problem solved	value created

operating expenses	sales goals	profits
◦	◦	◦
◦	◦	◦
◦	◦	◦
◦	◦	◦
◦	◦	◦
total	total	total

CHECKLIST
customer communication

- [ ] website
- [ ] email
- [ ] text
- [ ] phone call
- [ ] direct messages
- [ ] _____

PRESS RELEASE
outlets press release sent to:

LIST
how people describe me
- ◦
- ◦
- ◦
- ◦
- ◦

LIST
customer opinions
- ◦
- ◦
- ◦
- ◦
- ◦

LIST
events for customers
- ◦
- ◦
- ◦
- ◦
- ◦

LIST
things to learn
- ◦
- ◦
- ◦
- ◦
- ◦

LIST
inspirational brands
- ◦
- ◦
- ◦
- ◦
- ◦

LIST
favorite books & shows
- ◦
- ◦
- ◦
- ◦
- ◦

JOURNAL
how customers discover brand

AUDIO: **brand podcast**

VISUAL: **brand shows & live streams**

WRITE ARTICLES: **online & print media**

PRESS: **publicity plan & interviews**

COLLABORATIONS: **brands & influencers**

ADVERTISING: **types & placements**

MARKETING: **digital collateral**

MARKETING: **traditional collateral**

mission statement

daily goals

weekly goals

three month goals

one year goals

five year goals

ten year goals

JOURNAL

how's it going?

physically

intellectually

financially

socially

professionally

spiritually

relaxation levels

living space

LIST
expert skills

*
*
*
*
*

LIST
unique qualities

*
*
*
*
*

LIST
brand value to customers

*
*
*
*
*

LIST
achievements

*
*
*
*
*

LIST
vulnerabilities

*
*
*
*
*

revenue streams	problem solved	value created

operating expenses	sales goals	profits
◉	◉	◉
◉	◉	◉
◉	◉	◉
◉	◉	◉
◉	◉	◉
total	total	total

CHECKLIST
customer communication

PRESS RELEASE
outlets press release sent to:

- [ ] website
- [ ] email
- [ ] text
- [ ] phone call
- [ ] direct messages
- [ ]

LIST
how people describe me
- ◉
- ◉
- ◉
- ◉
- ◉

LIST
customer opinions
- ◉
- ◉
- ◉
- ◉
- ◉

LIST
events for customers
- ◉
- ◉
- ◉
- ◉
- ◉

LIST
things to learn
- ◉
- ◉
- ◉
- ◉
- ◉

LIST
inspirational brands
- ◉
- ◉
- ◉
- ◉
- ◉

LIST
favorite books & shows
- ◉
- ◉
- ◉
- ◉
- ◉

JOURNAL
how customers discover brand

AUDIO: **brand podcast**

VISUAL: **brand shows & live streams**

WRITE ARTICLES: **online & print media**

PRESS: **publicity plan & interviews**

COLLABORATIONS: **brands & influencers**

ADVERTISING: **types & placements**

MARKETING: **digital collateral**

MARKETING: **traditional collateral**

mission statement

daily goals

weekly goals

three month goals

one year goals

five year goals

ten year goals

JOURNAL
how's it going?

physically

intellectually

financially

socially

professionally

spiritually

relaxation levels

living space

LIST
expert skills

⊛
⊛
⊛
⊛
⊛

LIST
unique qualities

⊛
⊛
⊛
⊛
⊛

LIST
brand value to customers

⊛
⊛
⊛
⊛
⊛

LIST
achievements

⊛
⊛
⊛
⊛
⊛

LIST
vulnerabilities

⊛
⊛
⊛
⊛
⊛

revenue streams	problem solved	value created

operating expenses	sales goals	profits
●	●	●
●	●	●
●	●	●
●	●	●
●	●	●
total	total	total

CHECKLIST
customer communication

- website
- email
- text
- phone call
- direct messages

PRESS RELEASE
outlets press release sent to:

LIST
how people describe me
- ●
- ●
- ●
- ●
- ●

LIST
customer opinions
- ●
- ●
- ●
- ●
- ●

LIST
events for customers
- ●
- ●
- ●
- ●
- ●

LIST
things to learn
- ●
- ●
- ●
- ●
- ●

LIST
inspirational brands
- ●
- ●
- ●
- ●
- ●

LIST
favorite books & shows
- ●
- ●
- ●
- ●
- ●

JOURNAL
how customers discover brand

AUDIO: **brand podcast**

VISUAL: **brand shows & live streams**

WRITE ARTICLES: **online & print media**

PRESS: **publicity plan & interviews**

COLLABORATIONS: **brands & influencers**

ADVERTISING: **types & placements**

MARKETING: **digital collateral**

MARKETING: **traditional collateral**

mission statement

daily goals

weekly goals

three month goals

one year goals

five year goals

ten year goals

how's it going?

physically

intellectually

financially

socially

professionally

spiritually

relaxation levels

living space

LIST
expert skills

- ✷
- ✷
- ✷
- ✷
- ✷

LIST
unique qualities

- ✷
- ✷
- ✷
- ✷
- ✷

LIST
brand value to customers

- ✷
- ✷
- ✷
- ✷
- ✷

LIST
achievements

- ✷
- ✷
- ✷
- ✷
- ✷

LIST
vulnerabilities

- ✷
- ✷
- ✷
- ✷
- ✷

revenue streams	problem solved	value created

operating expenses	sales goals	profits
○	○	○
○	○	○
○	○	○
○	○	○
○	○	○
total	total	total

AUDIO: brand podcast

VISUAL: brand shows & live streams

WRITE ARTICLES: online & print media

PRESS: publicity plan & interviews

COLLABORATIONS: brands & influencers

ADVERTISING: types & placements

MARKETING: digital collateral

MARKETING: traditional collateral

CHECKLIST
customer communication

- website
- email
- text
- phone call
- direct messages

PRESS RELEASE
outlets press release sent to:

LIST
how people describe me
- ○
- ○
- ○
- ○
- ○

LIST
customer opinions
- ○
- ○
- ○
- ○
- ○

LIST
events for customers
- ○
- ○
- ○
- ○
- ○

LIST
things to learn
- ○
- ○
- ○
- ○
- ○

LIST
inspirational brands
- ○
- ○
- ○
- ○
- ○

LIST
favorite books & shows
- ○
- ○
- ○
- ○
- ○

mission statement

daily goals

weekly goals

three month goals

one year goals

five year goals

ten year goals

date _____

JOURNAL

how's it going?

physically

intellectually

financially

socially

professionally

spiritually

relaxation levels

living space

LIST
expert skills

LIST
unique qualities

LIST
brand value to customers

LIST
achievements

LIST
vulnerabilities

revenue streams	problem solved	value created

operating expenses	sales goals	profits
○	○	○
○	○	○
○	○	○
○	○	○
○	○	○
total	total	total

CHECKLIST
customer communication

- [ ] website
- [ ] email
- [ ] text
- [ ] phone call
- [ ] direct messages
- [ ]

PRESS RELEASE
outlets press release sent to:

LIST
how people describe me
- ○
- ○
- ○
- ○
- ○

LIST
customer opinions
- ○
- ○
- ○
- ○
- ○

LIST
events for customers
- ○
- ○
- ○
- ○
- ○

LIST
things to learn
- ○
- ○
- ○
- ○
- ○

LIST
inspirational brands
- ○
- ○
- ○
- ○
- ○

LIST
favorite books & shows
- ○
- ○
- ○
- ○
- ○

JOURNAL
how customers discover brand

AUDIO: **brand podcast**

VISUAL: **brand shows & live streams**

WRITE ARTICLES: **online & print media**

PRESS: **publicity plan & interviews**

COLLABORATIONS: **brands & influencers**

ADVERTISING: **types & placements**

MARKETING: **digital collateral**

MARKETING: **traditional collateral**

mission statement

daily goals

weekly goals

three month goals

one year goals

five year goals

ten year goals

JOURNAL

how's it going?

physically

intellectually

financially

socially

professionally

spiritually

relaxation levels

living space

LIST
expert skills

LIST
unique qualities

LIST
brand value to customers

LIST
achievements

LIST
vulnerabilities

revenue streams	problem solved	value created

operating expenses	sales goals	profits
•	•	•
•	•	•
•	•	•
•	•	•
•	•	•
total	total	total

JOURNAL
how customers discover brand

AUDIO: brand podcast

VISUAL: brand shows & live streams

WRITE ARTICLES: online & print media

PRESS: publicity plan & interviews

COLLABORATIONS: brands & influencers

ADVERTISING: types & placements

MARKETING: digital collateral

MARKETING: traditional collateral

CHECKLIST
customer communication

- [ ] website
- [ ] email
- [ ] text
- [ ] phone call
- [ ] direct messages
- [ ] _____

PRESS RELEASE
outlets press release sent to:

LIST
how people describe me
- •
- •
- •
- •
- •

LIST
customer opinions
- •
- •
- •
- •
- •

LIST
events for customers
- •
- •
- •
- •
- •

LIST
things to learn
- •
- •
- •
- •
- •

LIST
inspirational brands
- •
- •
- •
- •
- •

LIST
favorite books & shows
- •
- •
- •
- •
- •

mission statement

daily goals

weekly goals

three month goals

one year goals

five year goals

ten year goals

JOURNAL

how's it going?

physically

intellectually

financially

socially

professionally

spiritually

relaxation levels

living space

LIST
expert skills

-
-
-
-
-

LIST
unique qualities

-
-
-
-
-

LIST
brand value to customers

-
-
-
-
-

LIST
achievements

-
-
-
-
-

LIST
vulnerabilities

-
-
-
-
-

revenue streams	problem solved	value created

operating expenses	sales goals	profits
●	●	●
●	●	●
●	●	●
●	●	●
●	●	●
total	total	total

CHECKLIST
customer communication

- website
- email
- text
- phone call
- direct messages
- _____

PRESS RELEASE
outlets press release sent to:

LIST
how people describe me
- ●
- ●
- ●
- ●
- ●

LIST
customer opinions
- ●
- ●
- ●
- ●
- ●

LIST
events for customers
- ●
- ●
- ●
- ●
- ●

LIST
things to learn
- ●
- ●
- ●
- ●
- ●

LIST
inspirational brands
- ●
- ●
- ●
- ●
- ●

LIST
favorite books & shows
- ●
- ●
- ●
- ●
- ●

JOURNAL
how customers discover brand

AUDIO: **brand podcast**

VISUAL: **brand shows & live streams**

WRITE ARTICLES: **online & print media**

PRESS: **publicity plan & interviews**

COLLABORATIONS: **brands & influencers**

ADVERTISING: **types & placements**

MARKETING: **digital collateral**

MARKETING: **traditional collateral**

mission statement

daily goals

weekly goals

three month goals

one year goals

five year goals

ten year goals

JOURNAL

how's it going?

physically

intellectually

financially

socially

professionally

spiritually

relaxation levels

living space

LIST
expert skills

- ●
- ●
- ●
- ●
- ●

LIST
unique qualities

- ●
- ●
- ●
- ●
- ●

LIST
brand value to customers

- ●
- ●
- ●
- ●
- ●

LIST
achievements

- ●
- ●
- ●
- ●
- ●

LIST
vulnerabilities

- ●
- ●
- ●
- ●
- ●

revenue streams	problem solved	value created

JOURNAL
how customers discover brand

AUDIO: brand podcast

operating expenses	sales goals	profits
○	○	○
○	○	○
○	○	○
○	○	○
○	○	○
total	total	total

VISUAL: brand shows & live streams

WRITE ARTICLES: online & print media

CHECKLIST
customer communication

PRESS RELEASE
outlets press release sent to:

- [ ] website
- [ ] email
- [ ] text
- [ ] phone call
- [ ] direct messages
- [ ] _____

PRESS: publicity plan & interviews

COLLABORATIONS: brands & influencers

LIST
how people describe me

LIST
customer opinions

LIST
events for customers

- ○
- ○
- ○
- ○
- ○

ADVERTISING: types & placements

LIST
things to learn

LIST
inspirational brands

LIST
favorite books & shows

- ○
- ○
- ○
- ○
- ○

MARKETING: digital collateral

MARKETING: traditional collateral

mission statement

daily goals

weekly goals

three month goals

one year goals

five year goals

ten year goals

JOURNAL

how's it going?

physically

intellectually

financially

socially

professionally

spiritually

relaxation levels

living space

LIST
expert skills

-
-
-
-
-

LIST
unique qualities

-
-
-
-
-

LIST
brand value to customers

-
-
-
-
-

LIST
achievements

-
-
-
-
-

LIST
vulnerabilities

-
-
-
-
-

revenue streams	problem solved	value created

operating expenses	sales goals	profits
total	total	total

CHECKLIST
customer communication

- website
- email
- text
- phone call
- direct messages
- _____

PRESS RELEASE
outlets press release sent to:

LIST
how people describe me

-
-
-
-
-

LIST
customer opinions

-
-
-
-
-

LIST
events for customers

-
-
-
-
-

LIST
things to learn

-
-
-
-
-

LIST
inspirational brands

-
-
-
-
-

LIST
favorite books & shows

-
-
-
-
-

JOURNAL
how customers discover brand

AUDIO: brand podcast

VISUAL: brand shows & live streams

WRITE ARTICLES: online & print media

PRESS: publicity plan & interviews

COLLABORATIONS: brands & influencers

ADVERTISING: types & placements

MARKETING: digital collateral

MARKETING: traditional collateral

mission statement

daily goals

weekly goals

three month goals

one year goals

five year goals

ten year goals

date _____

JOURNAL

how's it going?

physically

intellectually

financially

socially

professionally

spiritually

relaxation levels

living space

LIST
expert skills

- ○
- ○
- ○
- ○
- ○

LIST
unique qualities

- ○
- ○
- ○
- ○
- ○

LIST
brand value to customers

- ○
- ○
- ○
- ○
- ○

LIST
achievements

- ○
- ○
- ○
- ○
- ○

LIST
vulnerabilities

- ○
- ○
- ○
- ○
- ○

revenue streams	problem solved	value created

operating expenses	sales goals	profits
●	●	●
●	●	●
●	●	●
●	●	●
●	●	●
total	total	total

CHECKLIST
customer communication

PRESS RELEASE
outlets press release sent to:

- [ ] website
- [ ] email
- [ ] text
- [ ] phone call
- [ ] direct messages
- [ ] _____

LIST
how people describe me
- ●
- ●
- ●
- ●
- ●

LIST
customer opinions
- ●
- ●
- ●
- ●
- ●

LIST
events for customers
- ●
- ●
- ●
- ●
- ●

LIST
things to learn
- ●
- ●
- ●
- ●
- ●

LIST
inspirational brands
- ●
- ●
- ●
- ●
- ●

LIST
favorite books & shows
- ●
- ●
- ●
- ●
- ●

JOURNAL
how customers discover brand

AUDIO: **brand podcast**

VISUAL: **brand shows & live streams**

WRITE ARTICLES: **online & print media**

PRESS: **publicity plan & interviews**

COLLABORATIONS: **brands & influencers**

ADVERTISING: **types & placements**

MARKETING: **digital collateral**

MARKETING: **traditional collateral**

mission statement

daily goals

weekly goals

three month goals

one year goals

five year goals

ten year goals

JOURNAL

how's it going?

physically

intellectually

financially

socially

professionally

spiritually

relaxation levels

living space

LIST
expert skills

*
*
*
*
*

LIST
unique qualities

*
*
*
*
*

LIST
brand value to customers

*
*
*
*
*

LIST
achievements

*
*
*
*
*

LIST
vulnerabilities

*
*
*
*
*

revenue streams	problem solved	value created

operating expenses	sales goals	profits
⊙	⊙	⊙
⊙	⊙	⊙
⊙	⊙	⊙
⊙	⊙	⊙
⊙	⊙	⊙
total	total	total

CHECKLIST
customer communication

- [ ] website
- [ ] email
- [ ] text
- [ ] phone call
- [ ] direct messages
- [ ] _____

PRESS RELEASE
outlets press release sent to:

LIST
how people describe me
- ⊙
- ⊙
- ⊙
- ⊙
- ⊙

LIST
customer opinions
- ⊙
- ⊙
- ⊙
- ⊙
- ⊙

LIST
events for customers
- ⊙
- ⊙
- ⊙
- ⊙
- ⊙

LIST
things to learn
- ⊙
- ⊙
- ⊙
- ⊙
- ⊙

LIST
inspirational brands
- ⊙
- ⊙
- ⊙
- ⊙
- ⊙

LIST
favorite books & shows
- ⊙
- ⊙
- ⊙
- ⊙
- ⊙

JOURNAL
how customers discover brand

AUDIO: brand podcast

VISUAL: brand shows & live streams

WRITE ARTICLES: online & print media

PRESS: publicity plan & interviews

COLLABORATIONS: brands & influencers

ADVERTISING: types & placements

MARKETING: digital collateral

MARKETING: traditional collateral

mission statement

daily goals

weekly goals

three month goals

one year goals

five year goals

ten year goals

JOURNAL

how's it going?

physically

intellectually

financially

socially

professionally

spiritually

relaxation levels

living space

LIST
expert skills

- ○
- ○
- ○
- ○
- ○

LIST
unique qualities

- ○
- ○
- ○
- ○
- ○

LIST
brand value to customers

- ○
- ○
- ○
- ○
- ○

LIST
achievements

- ○
- ○
- ○
- ○
- ○

LIST
vulnerabilities

- ○
- ○
- ○
- ○
- ○

revenue streams	problem solved	value created

operating expenses	sales goals	profits
○	○	○
○	○	○
○	○	○
○	○	○
○	○	○
total	total	total

CHECKLIST
customer communication

- website
- email
- text
- phone call
- direct messages
-

PRESS RELEASE
outlets press release sent to:

LIST
how people describe me
- ○
- ○
- ○
- ○
- ○

LIST
customer opinions
- ○
- ○
- ○
- ○
- ○

LIST
events for customers
- ○
- ○
- ○
- ○
- ○

LIST
things to learn
- ○
- ○
- ○
- ○
- ○

LIST
inspirational brands
- ○
- ○
- ○
- ○
- ○

LIST
favorite books & shows
- ○
- ○
- ○
- ○
- ○

JOURNAL
how customers discover brand

AUDIO: brand podcast

VISUAL: brand shows & live streams

WRITE ARTICLES: online & print media

PRESS: publicity plan & interviews

COLLABORATIONS: brands & influencers

ADVERTISING: types & placements

MARKETING: digital collateral

MARKETING: traditional collateral

mission statement

daily goals

weekly goals

three month goals

one year goals

five year goals

ten year goals

JOURNAL

how's it going?

physically

intellectually

financially

socially

professionally

spiritually

relaxation levels

living space

LIST
expert skills

LIST
unique qualities

LIST
brand value to customers

LIST
achievements

LIST
vulnerabilities

revenue streams	problem solved	value created

operating expenses	sales goals	profits
○	○	○
○	○	○
○	○	○
○	○	○
○	○	○
total	total	total

CHECKLIST
customer communication

☐ website

☐ email

☐ text

☐ phone call

☐ direct messages

☐

PRESS RELEASE
outlets press release sent to:

LIST
how people describe me
- ○
- ○
- ○
- ○
- ○

LIST
customer opinions
- ○
- ○
- ○
- ○
- ○

LIST
events for customers
- ○
- ○
- ○
- ○
- ○

LIST
things to learn
- ○
- ○
- ○
- ○
- ○

LIST
inspirational brands
- ○
- ○
- ○
- ○
- ○

LIST
favorite books & shows
- ○
- ○
- ○
- ○
- ○

JOURNAL
how customers discover brand

AUDIO: **brand podcast**

VISUAL: **brand shows & live streams**

WRITE ARTICLES: **online & print media**

PRESS: **publicity plan & interviews**

COLLABORATIONS: **brands & influencers**

ADVERTISING: **types & placements**

MARKETING: **digital collateral**

MARKETING: **traditional collateral**

mission statement

daily goals

weekly goals

three month goals

one year goals

five year goals

ten year goals

JOURNAL

how's it going?

physically

intellectually

financially

socially

professionally

spiritually

relaxation levels

living space

LIST
expert skills

-
-
-
-
-

LIST
unique qualities

-
-
-
-
-

LIST
brand value to customers

-
-
-
-
-

LIST
achievements

-
-
-
-

LIST
vulnerabilities

-
-
-
-
-

revenue streams	problem solved	value created

operating expenses	sales goals	profits
○	○	○
○	○	○
○	○	○
○	○	○
○	○	○
total	total	total

CHECKLIST
customer communication

- website
- email
- text
- phone call
- direct messages

PRESS RELEASE
outlets press release sent to:

LIST
how people describe me

- ○
- ○
- ○
- ○
- ○

LIST
customer opinions

- ○
- ○
- ○
- ○
- ○

LIST
events for customers

- ○
- ○
- ○
- ○
- ○

LIST
things to learn

- ○
- ○
- ○
- ○
- ○

LIST
inspirational brands

- ○
- ○
- ○
- ○
- ○

LIST
favorite books & shows

- ○
- ○
- ○
- ○
- ○

JOURNAL
how customers discover brand

AUDIO: **brand podcast**

VISUAL: **brand shows & live streams**

WRITE ARTICLES: **online & print media**

PRESS: **publicity plan & interviews**

COLLABORATIONS: **brands & influencers**

ADVERTISING: **types & placements**

MARKETING: **digital collateral**

MARKETING: **traditional collateral**

mission statement

daily goals

weekly goals

three month goals

one year goals

five year goals

ten year goals

JOURNAL

how's it going?

physically

intellectually

financially

socially

professionally

spiritually

relaxation levels

living space

LIST
expert skills

- ●
- ●
- ●
- ●
- ●

LIST
unique qualities

- ●
- ●
- ●
- ●
- ●

LIST
brand value to customers

- ●
- ●
- ●
- ●
- ●

LIST
achievements

- ●
- ●
- ●
- ●
- ●

LIST
vulnerabilities

- ●
- ●
- ●
- ●
- ●

revenue streams	problem solved	value created

AUDIO: brand podcast

operating expenses	sales goals	profits
○	○	○
○	○	○
○	○	○
○	○	○
○	○	○
total	total	total

VISUAL: brand shows & live streams

WRITE ARTICLES: online & print media

CHECKLIST
customer communication

PRESS RELEASE
outlets press release sent to:

- website
- email
- text
- phone call
- direct messages

PRESS: publicity plan & interviews

COLLABORATIONS: brands & influencers

LIST
how people describe me
- ○
- ○
- ○
- ○
- ○

LIST
customer opinions
- ○
- ○
- ○
- ○
- ○

LIST
events for customers
- ○
- ○
- ○
- ○
- ○

ADVERTISING: types & placements

LIST
things to learn
- ○
- ○
- ○
- ○
- ○

LIST
inspirational brands
- ○
- ○
- ○
- ○
- ○

LIST
favorite books & shows
- ○
- ○
- ○
- ○
- ○

MARKETING: digital collateral

MARKETING: traditional collateral

mission statement

daily goals

weekly goals

three month goals

one year goals

five year goals

ten year goals

mission statement

JOURNAL

how's it going?

physically

intellectually

financially

socially

professionally

spiritually

relaxation levels

living space

LIST
expert skills

LIST
unique qualities

LIST
brand value to customers

LIST
achievements

LIST
vulnerabilities

revenue streams	problem solved	value created

operating expenses	sales goals	profits
⚬	⚬	⚬
⚬	⚬	⚬
⚬	⚬	⚬
⚬	⚬	⚬
⚬	⚬	⚬
total	total	total

CHECKLIST
customer communication

- [ ] website
- [ ] email
- [ ] text
- [ ] phone call
- [ ] direct messages
- [ ]

PRESS RELEASE
outlets press release sent to:

LIST
how people describe me
- ⚬
- ⚬
- ⚬
- ⚬
- ⚬

LIST
customer opinions
- ⚬
- ⚬
- ⚬
- ⚬
- ⚬

LIST
events for customers
- ⚬
- ⚬
- ⚬
- ⚬
- ⚬

LIST
things to learn
- ⚬
- ⚬
- ⚬
- ⚬
- ⚬

LIST
inspirational brands
- ⚬
- ⚬
- ⚬
- ⚬
- ⚬

LIST
favorite books & shows
- ⚬
- ⚬
- ⚬
- ⚬
- ⚬

JOURNAL
how customers discover brand

AUDIO: **brand podcast**

VISUAL: **brand shows & live streams**

WRITE ARTICLES: **online & print media**

PRESS: **publicity plan & interviews**

COLLABORATIONS: **brands & influencers**

ADVERTISING: **types & placements**

MARKETING: **digital collateral**

MARKETING: **traditional collateral**

mission statement

daily goals

weekly goals

three month goals

one year goals

five year goals

ten year goals

JOURNAL

how's it going?

physically

intellectually

financially

socially

professionally

spiritually

relaxation levels

living space

LIST
expert skills

- ◉
- ◉
- ◉
- ◉
- ◉

LIST
unique qualities

- ◉
- ◉
- ◉
- ◉
- ◉

LIST
brand value to customers

- ◉
- ◉
- ◉
- ◉
- ◉

LIST
achievements

- ◉
- ◉
- ◉
- ◉
- ◉

LIST
vulnerabilities

- ◉
- ◉
- ◉
- ◉
- ◉

revenue streams	problem solved	value created

operating expenses	sales goals	profits
⊚	⊚	⊚
⊚	⊚	⊚
⊚	⊚	⊚
⊚	⊚	⊚
⊚	⊚	⊚
total	total	total

CHECKLIST
customer communication

☐ website

☐ email

☐ text

☐ phone call

☐ direct messages

☐

PRESS RELEASE
outlets press release sent to:

LIST
how people describe me

⊚

⊚

⊚

⊚

⊚

LIST
customer opinions

⊚

⊚

⊚

⊚

⊚

LIST
events for customers

⊚

⊚

⊚

⊚

⊚

LIST
things to learn

⊚

⊚

⊚

⊚

⊚

LIST
inspirational brands

⊚

⊚

⊚

⊚

⊚

LIST
favorite books & shows

⊚

⊚

⊚

⊚

⊚

JOURNAL
how customers discover brand

AUDIO: brand podcast

VISUAL: brand shows & live streams

WRITE ARTICLES: online & print media

PRESS: publicity plan & interviews

COLLABORATIONS: brands & influencers

ADVERTISING: types & placements

MARKETING: digital collateral

MARKETING: traditional collateral

mission statement

daily goals

weekly goals

three month goals

one year goals

five year goals

ten year goals

date _____

JOURNAL

how's it going?

physically

intellectually

financially

socially

professionally

spiritually

relaxation levels

living space

LIST
expert skills

- ○
- ○
- ○
- ○
- ○

LIST
unique qualities

- ○
- ○
- ○
- ○
- ○

LIST
brand value to customers

- ○
- ○
- ○
- ○
- ○

LIST
achievements

- ○
- ○
- ○
- ○
- ○

LIST
vulnerabilities

- ○
- ○
- ○
- ○
- ○

revenue streams	problem solved	value created

operating expenses	sales goals	profits
○	○	○
○	○	○
○	○	○
○	○	○
○	○	○
total	total	total

CHECKLIST
customer communication

☐ website
☐ email
☐ text
☐ phone call
☐ direct messages
☐

PRESS RELEASE
outlets press release sent to:

LIST
how people describe me
○
○
○
○
○

LIST
customer opinions
○
○
○
○
○

LIST
events for customers
○
○
○
○
○

LIST
things to learn
○
○
○
○
○

LIST
inspirational brands
○
○
○
○
○

LIST
favorite books & shows
○
○
○
○
○

JOURNAL
how customers discover brand

AUDIO: **brand podcast**

VISUAL: **brand shows & live streams**

WRITE ARTICLES: **online & print media**

PRESS: **publicity plan & interviews**

COLLABORATIONS: **brands & influencers**

ADVERTISING: **types & placements**

MARKETING: **digital collateral**

MARKETING: **traditional collateral**

mission statement

daily goals

weekly goals

three month goals

one year goals

five year goals

ten year goals

JOURNAL

how's it going?

physically

intellectually

financially

socially

professionally

spiritually

relaxation levels

living space

LIST
expert skills

- ⚬
- ⚬
- ⚬
- ⚬
- ⚬

LIST
unique qualities

- ⚬
- ⚬
- ⚬
- ⚬
- ⚬

LIST
brand value to customers

- ⚬
- ⚬
- ⚬
- ⚬
- ⚬

LIST
achievements

- ⚬
- ⚬
- ⚬
- ⚬
- ⚬

LIST
vulnerabilities

- ⚬
- ⚬
- ⚬
- ⚬
- ⚬

revenue streams	problem solved	value created

operating expenses	sales goals	profits
◉	◉	◉
◉	◉	◉
◉	◉	◉
◉	◉	◉
◉	◉	◉
total	total	total

CHECKLIST
customer communication

- website
- email
- text
- phone call
- direct messages
- _____

PRESS RELEASE
outlets press release sent to:

LIST
how people describe me
- ◉
- ◉
- ◉
- ◉
- ◉

LIST
customer opinions
- ◉
- ◉
- ◉
- ◉
- ◉

LIST
events for customers
- ◉
- ◉
- ◉
- ◉
- ◉

LIST
things to learn
- ◉
- ◉
- ◉
- ◉
- ◉

LIST
inspirational brands
- ◉
- ◉
- ◉
- ◉
- ◉

LIST
favorite books & shows
- ◉
- ◉
- ◉
- ◉
- ◉

JOURNAL
how customers discover brand

AUDIO: brand podcast

VISUAL: brand shows & live streams

WRITE ARTICLES: online & print media

PRESS: publicity plan & interviews

COLLABORATIONS: brands & influencers

ADVERTISING: types & placements

MARKETING: digital collateral

MARKETING: traditional collateral

mission statement

daily goals

weekly goals

three month goals

one year goals

five year goals

ten year goals

---

date _____

how's it going?

physically

intellectually

financially

socially

professionally

spiritually

relaxation levels

living space

LIST
expert skills

- ⚬
- ⚬
- ⚬
- ⚬
- ⚬

LIST
unique qualities

- ⚬
- ⚬
- ⚬
- ⚬
- ⚬

LIST
brand value to customers

- ⚬
- ⚬
- ⚬
- ⚬
- ⚬

LIST
achievements

- ⚬
- ⚬
- ⚬
- ⚬
- ⚬

LIST
vulnerabilities

- ⚬
- ⚬
- ⚬
- ⚬
- ⚬

revenue streams	problem solved	value created

operating expenses	sales goals	profits
○	○	○
○	○	○
○	○	○
○	○	○
○	○	○
total	total	total

CHECKLIST
customer communication

- [ ] website
- [ ] email
- [ ] text
- [ ] phone call
- [ ] direct messages
- [ ]

PRESS RELEASE
outlets press release sent to:

LIST
how people describe me
- ○
- ○
- ○
- ○
- ○

LIST
customer opinions
- ○
- ○
- ○
- ○
- ○

LIST
events for customers
- ○
- ○
- ○
- ○
- ○

LIST
things to learn
- ○
- ○
- ○
- ○
- ○

LIST
inspirational brands
- ○
- ○
- ○
- ○
- ○

LIST
favorite books & shows
- ○
- ○
- ○
- ○
- ○

JOURNAL
how customers discover brand

AUDIO: **brand podcast**

VISUAL: **brand shows & live streams**

WRITE ARTICLES: **online & print media**

PRESS: **publicity plan & interviews**

COLLABORATIONS: **brands & influencers**

ADVERTISING: **types & placements**

MARKETING: **digital collateral**

MARKETING: **traditional collateral**

mission statement

daily goals

weekly goals

three month goals

one year goals

five year goals

ten year goals

JOURNAL

how's it going?

physically

intellectually

financially

socially

professionally

spiritually

relaxation levels

living space

LIST
expert skills

- ·
- ·
- ·
- ·
- ·

LIST
unique qualities

- ·
- ·
- ·
- ·
- ·

LIST
brand value to customers

- ·
- ·
- ·
- ·
- ·

LIST
achievements

- ·
- ·
- ·
- ·
- ·

LIST
vulnerabilities

- ·
- ·
- ·
- ·

revenue streams	problem solved	value created

operating expenses	sales goals	profits
○	○	○
○	○	○
○	○	○
○	○	○
○	○	○
total	total	total

CHECKLIST
customer communication

- [ ] website
- [ ] email
- [ ] text
- [ ] phone call
- [ ] direct messages
- [ ]

PRESS RELEASE
outlets press release sent to:

LIST
how people describe me
- ○
- ○
- ○
- ○
- ○

LIST
customer opinions
- ○
- ○
- ○
- ○
- ○

LIST
events for customers
- ○
- ○
- ○
- ○
- ○

LIST
things to learn
- ○
- ○
- ○
- ○
- ○

LIST
inspirational brands
- ○
- ○
- ○
- ○
- ○

LIST
favorite books & shows
- ○
- ○
- ○
- ○
- ○

JOURNAL
how customers discover brand

AUDIO: **brand podcast**

VISUAL: **brand shows & live streams**

WRITE ARTICLES: **online & print media**

PRESS: **publicity plan & interviews**

COLLABORATIONS: **brands & influencers**

ADVERTISING: **types & placements**

MARKETING: **digital collateral**

MARKETING: **traditional collateral**

mission statement

daily goals

weekly goals

three month goals

one year goals

five year goals

ten year goals

date _____

JOURNAL

how's it going?

physically

intellectually

financially

socially

professionally

spiritually

relaxation levels

living space

LIST
expert skills

*
*
*
*
*

LIST
unique qualities

*
*
*
*
*

LIST
brand value to customers

*
*
*
*
*

LIST
achievements

*
*
*
*
*

LIST
vulnerabilities

*
*
*
*
*

revenue streams	problem solved	value created

operating expenses	sales goals	profits
○	○	○
○	○	○
○	○	○
○	○	○
○	○	○
total	total	total

CHECKLIST
customer communication

- [ ] website
- [ ] email
- [ ] text
- [ ] phone call
- [ ] direct messages
- [ ]

PRESS RELEASE
outlets press release sent to:

LIST
how people describe me

- ○
- ○
- ○
- ○
- ○

LIST
customer opinions

- ○
- ○
- ○
- ○
- ○

LIST
events for customers

- ○
- ○
- ○
- ○
- ○

LIST
things to learn

- ○
- ○
- ○
- ○
- ○

LIST
inspirational brands

- ○
- ○
- ○
- ○
- ○

LIST
favorite books & shows

- ○
- ○
- ○
- ○
- ○

JOURNAL
how customers discover brand

AUDIO: **brand podcast**

VISUAL: **brand shows & live streams**

WRITE ARTICLES: **online & print media**

PRESS: **publicity plan & interviews**

COLLABORATIONS: **brands & influencers**

ADVERTISING: **types & placements**

MARKETING: **digital collateral**

MARKETING: **traditional collateral**

mission statement

daily goals

weekly goals

three month goals

one year goals

five year goals

ten year goals

JOURNAL

how's it going?

physically

intellectually

financially

socially

professionally

spiritually

relaxation levels

living space

LIST
expert skills

LIST
unique qualities

LIST
brand value to customers

LIST
achievements

LIST
vulnerabilities

revenue streams	problem solved	value created

operating expenses	sales goals	profits
○	○	○
○	○	○
○	○	○
○	○	○
○	○	○
total	total	total

CHECKLIST
customer communication

- [ ] website
- [ ] email
- [ ] text
- [ ] phone call
- [ ] direct messages
- [ ]

PRESS RELEASE
outlets press release sent to:

LIST
how people describe me
- ○
- ○
- ○
- ○
- ○

LIST
customer opinions
- ○
- ○
- ○
- ○
- ○

LIST
events for customers
- ○
- ○
- ○
- ○
- ○

LIST
things to learn
- ○
- ○
- ○
- ○
- ○

LIST
inspirational brands
- ○
- ○
- ○
- ○
- ○

LIST
favorite books & shows
- ○
- ○
- ○
- ○
- ○

JOURNAL
how customers discover brand

AUDIO: **brand podcast**

VISUAL: **brand shows & live streams**

WRITE ARTICLES: **online & print media**

PRESS: **publicity plan & interviews**

COLLABORATIONS: **brands & influencers**

ADVERTISING: **types & placements**

MARKETING: **digital collateral**

MARKETING: **traditional collateral**

mission statement

daily goals

weekly goals

three month goals

one year goals

five year goals

ten year goals

mission statement

mission statement

date _____

JOURNAL

how's it going?

physically

intellectually

financially

socially

professionally

spiritually

relaxation levels

living space

LIST
expert skills
- ⚬
- ⚬
- ⚬
- ⚬
- ⚬

LIST
unique qualities
- ⚬
- ⚬
- ⚬
- ⚬
- ⚬

LIST
brand value to customers
- ⚬
- ⚬
- ⚬
- ⚬
- ⚬

LIST
achievements
- ⚬
- ⚬
- ⚬
- ⚬
- ⚬

LIST
vulnerabilities
- ⚬
- ⚬
- ⚬
- ⚬
- ⚬

revenue streams	problem solved	value created

operating expenses	sales goals	profits
○	○	○
○	○	○
○	○	○
○	○	○
○	○	○
total	total	total

CHECKLIST
customer communication

- website
- email
- text
- phone call
- direct messages
-

PRESS RELEASE
outlets press release sent to:

LIST
how people describe me
- ○
- ○
- ○
- ○
- ○

LIST
customer opinions
- ○
- ○
- ○
- ○
- ○

LIST
events for customers
- ○
- ○
- ○
- ○
- ○

LIST
things to learn
- ○
- ○
- ○
- ○
- ○

LIST
inspirational brands
- ○
- ○
- ○
- ○
- ○

LIST
favorite books & shows
- ○
- ○
- ○
- ○
- ○

JOURNAL
how customers discover brand

AUDIO: **brand podcast**

VISUAL: **brand shows & live streams**

WRITE ARTICLES: **online & print media**

PRESS: **publicity plan & interviews**

COLLABORATIONS: **brands & influencers**

ADVERTISING: **types & placements**

MARKETING: **digital collateral**

MARKETING: **traditional collateral**

mission statement

daily goals

weekly goals

three month goals

one year goals

five year goals

ten year goals

JOURNAL

how's it going?

physically

intellectually

financially

socially

professionally

spiritually

relaxation levels

living space

LIST
expert skills

LIST
unique qualities

LIST
brand value to customers

LIST
achievements

LIST
vulnerabilities

revenue streams	problem solved	value created

operating expenses	sales goals	profits
○	○	○
○	○	○
○	○	○
○	○	○
○	○	○
total	total	total

AUDIO: brand podcast

VISUAL: brand shows & live streams

WRITE ARTICLES: online & print media

CHECKLIST
customer communication

☐ website

☐ email

☐ text

☐ phone call

☐ direct messages

☐

PRESS RELEASE
outlets press release sent to:

PRESS: publicity plan & interviews

COLLABORATIONS: brands & influencers

LIST how people describe me	LIST customer opinions	LIST events for customers
○	○	○
○	○	○
○	○	○
○	○	○
○	○	○

ADVERTISING: types & placements

LIST things to learn	LIST inspirational brands	LIST favorite books & shows
○	○	○
○	○	○
○	○	○
○	○	○
○	○	○

MARKETING: digital collateral

MARKETING: traditional collateral

mission statement

daily goals

weekly goals

three month goals

one year goals

five year goals

ten year goals

mission statement

date _____

JOURNAL

how's it going?

physically

intellectually

financially

socially

professionally

spiritually

relaxation levels

living space

LIST
expert skills
- ✦
- ✦
- ✦
- ✦
- ✦

LIST
unique qualities
- ✦
- ✦
- ✦
- ✦
- ✦

LIST
brand value to customers
- ✦
- ✦
- ✦
- ✦
- ✦

LIST
achievements
- ✦
- ✦
- ✦
- ✦
- ✦

LIST
vulnerabilities
- ✦
- ✦
- ✦
- ✦
- ✦

revenue streams	problem solved	value created

operating expenses	sales goals	profits
◦	◦	◦
◦	◦	◦
◦	◦	◦
◦	◦	◦
◦	◦	◦
total	total	total

JOURNAL
how customers discover brand

AUDIO: brand podcast

VISUAL: brand shows & live streams

WRITE ARTICLES: online & print media

PRESS: publicity plan & interviews

COLLABORATIONS: brands & influencers

ADVERTISING: types & placements

MARKETING: digital collateral

MARKETING: traditional collateral

CHECKLIST
customer communication

- website
- email
- text
- phone call
- direct messages

PRESS RELEASE
outlets press release sent to:

LIST
how people describe me

- ◦
- ◦
- ◦
- ◦
- ◦

LIST
customer opinions

- ◦
- ◦
- ◦
- ◦
- ◦

LIST
events for customers

- ◦
- ◦
- ◦
- ◦
- ◦

LIST
things to learn

- ◦
- ◦
- ◦
- ◦
- ◦

LIST
inspirational brands

- ◦
- ◦
- ◦
- ◦
- ◦

LIST
favorite books & shows

- ◦
- ◦
- ◦
- ◦
- ◦

mission statement

daily goals

weekly goals

three month goals

one year goals

five year goals

ten year goals

mission statement

JOURNAL

how's it going?

physically

intellectually

financially

socially

professionally

spiritually

relaxation levels

living space

LIST
expert skills

LIST
unique qualities

LIST
brand value to customers

LIST
achievements

LIST
vulnerabilities

revenue streams	problem solved	value created

operating expenses	sales goals	profits
○	○	○
○	○	○
○	○	○
○	○	○
○	○	○
total	total	total

CHECKLIST
customer communication

- website
- email
- text
- phone call
- direct messages

PRESS RELEASE
outlets press release sent to:

LIST
how people describe me
- ○
- ○
- ○
- ○
- ○

LIST
customer opinions
- ○
- ○
- ○
- ○
- ○

LIST
events for customers
- ○
- ○
- ○
- ○
- ○

LIST
things to learn
- ○
- ○
- ○
- ○
- ○

LIST
inspirational brands
- ○
- ○
- ○
- ○
- ○

LIST
favorite books & shows
- ○
- ○
- ○
- ○
- ○

JOURNAL
how customers discover brand

AUDIO: **brand podcast**

VISUAL: **brand shows & live streams**

WRITE ARTICLES: **online & print media**

PRESS: **publicity plan & interviews**

COLLABORATIONS: **brands & influencers**

ADVERTISING: **types & placements**

MARKETING: **digital collateral**

MARKETING: **traditional collateral**

mission statement

daily goals

weekly goals

three month goals

one year goals

five year goals

ten year goals

JOURNAL

how's it going?

physically

intellectually

financially

socially

professionally

spiritually

relaxation levels

living space

LIST
expert skills

LIST
unique qualities

LIST
brand value to customers

LIST
achievements

LIST
vulnerabilities

revenue streams	problem solved	value created

operating expenses	sales goals	profits
⊙	⊙	⊙
⊙	⊙	⊙
⊙	⊙	⊙
⊙	⊙	⊙
⊙	⊙	⊙
total	total	total

CHECKLIST
customer communication

- [ ] website
- [ ] email
- [ ] text
- [ ] phone call
- [ ] direct messages
- [ ]

PRESS RELEASE
outlets press release sent to:

LIST
how people describe me

- ⊙
- ⊙
- ⊙
- ⊙
- ⊙

LIST
customer opinions

- ⊙
- ⊙
- ⊙
- ⊙
- ⊙

LIST
events for customers

- ⊙
- ⊙
- ⊙
- ⊙
- ⊙

LIST
things to learn

- ⊙
- ⊙
- ⊙
- ⊙
- ⊙

LIST
inspirational brands

- ⊙
- ⊙
- ⊙
- ⊙
- ⊙

LIST
favorite books & shows

- ⊙
- ⊙
- ⊙
- ⊙
- ⊙

JOURNAL
how customers discover brand

AUDIO: brand podcast

VISUAL: brand shows & live streams

WRITE ARTICLES: online & print media

PRESS: publicity plan & interviews

COLLABORATIONS: brands & influencers

ADVERTISING: types & placements

MARKETING: digital collateral

MARKETING: traditional collateral

mission statement

daily goals

weekly goals

three month goals

one year goals

five year goals

ten year goals

date _____

how's it going?

physically

intellectually

financially

socially

professionally

spiritually

relaxation levels

living space

LIST
expert skills

LIST
unique qualities

LIST
brand value to customers

LIST
achievements

LIST
vulnerabilities

revenue streams	problem solved	value created

operating expenses	sales goals	profits
○	○	○
○	○	○
○	○	○
○	○	○
○	○	○
total	total	total

CHECKLIST
customer communication

- [ ] website
- [ ] email
- [ ] text
- [ ] phone call
- [ ] direct messages
- [ ] _____

PRESS RELEASE
outlets press release sent to:

LIST
how people describe me
- ○
- ○
- ○
- ○
- ○

LIST
customer opinions
- ○
- ○
- ○
- ○
- ○

LIST
events for customers
- ○
- ○
- ○
- ○
- ○

LIST
things to learn
- ○
- ○
- ○
- ○
- ○

LIST
inspirational brands
- ○
- ○
- ○
- ○
- ○

LIST
favorite books & shows
- ○
- ○
- ○
- ○
- ○

JOURNAL
how customers discover brand

AUDIO: brand podcast

VISUAL: brand shows & live streams

WRITE ARTICLES: online & print media

PRESS: publicity plan & interviews

COLLABORATIONS: brands & influencers

ADVERTISING: types & placements

MARKETING: digital collateral

MARKETING: traditional collateral

mission statement

daily goals

weekly goals

three month goals

one year goals

five year goals

ten year goals

JOURNAL

how's it going?

physically

intellectually

financially

socially

professionally

spiritually

relaxation levels

living space

LIST
expert skills

- ◦
- ◦
- ◦
- ◦
- ◦

LIST
unique qualities

- ◦
- ◦
- ◦
- ◦
- ◦

LIST
brand value to customers

- ◦
- ◦
- ◦
- ◦
- ◦

LIST
achievements

- ◦
- ◦
- ◦
- ◦
- ◦

LIST
vulnerabilities

- ◦
- ◦
- ◦
- ◦
- ◦

revenue streams	problem solved	value created

operating expenses	sales goals	profits
⬚	⬚	⬚
⬚	⬚	⬚
⬚	⬚	⬚
⬚	⬚	⬚
⬚	⬚	⬚
total	total	total

CHECKLIST
customer communication

- ⬚ website
- ⬚ email
- ⬚ text
- ⬚ phone call
- ⬚ direct messages
- ⬚

PRESS RELEASE
outlets press release sent to:

LIST
how people describe me
- ⬚
- ⬚
- ⬚
- ⬚
- ⬚

LIST
customer opinions
- ⬚
- ⬚
- ⬚
- ⬚
- ⬚

LIST
events for customers
- ⬚
- ⬚
- ⬚
- ⬚
- ⬚

LIST
things to learn
- ⬚
- ⬚
- ⬚
- ⬚
- ⬚

LIST
inspirational brands
- ⬚
- ⬚
- ⬚
- ⬚
- ⬚

LIST
favorite books & shows
- ⬚
- ⬚
- ⬚
- ⬚
- ⬚

JOURNAL
how customers discover brand

AUDIO: **brand podcast**

VISUAL: **brand shows & live streams**

WRITE ARTICLES: **online & print media**

PRESS: **publicity plan & interviews**

COLLABORATIONS: **brands & influencers**

ADVERTISING: **types & placements**

MARKETING: **digital collateral**

MARKETING: **traditional collateral**

mission statement

daily goals

weekly goals

three month goals

one year goals

five year goals

ten year goals

JOURNAL
how's it going?

physically

intellectually

financially

socially

professionally

spiritually

relaxation levels

living space

LIST
expert skills

- ⬡
- ⬡
- ⬡
- ⬡
- ⬡

LIST
unique qualities

- ⬡
- ⬡
- ⬡
- ⬡
- ⬡

LIST
brand value to customers

- ⬡
- ⬡
- ⬡
- ⬡
- ⬡

LIST
achievements

- ⬡
- ⬡
- ⬡
- ⬡
- ⬡

LIST
vulnerabilities

- ⬡
- ⬡
- ⬡
- ⬡
- ⬡

revenue streams	problem solved	value created

operating expenses	sales goals	profits
○	○	○
○	○	○
○	○	○
○	○	○
○	○	○
total	total	total

CHECKLIST
customer communication

- [ ] website
- [ ] email
- [ ] text
- [ ] phone call
- [ ] direct messages
- [ ] _____

PRESS RELEASE
outlets press release sent to:

LIST
how people describe me
- ○
- ○
- ○
- ○
- ○

LIST
customer opinions
- ○
- ○
- ○
- ○
- ○

LIST
events for customers
- ○
- ○
- ○
- ○
- ○

LIST
things to learn
- ○
- ○
- ○
- ○
- ○

LIST
inspirational brands
- ○
- ○
- ○
- ○
- ○

LIST
favorite books & shows
- ○
- ○
- ○
- ○
- ○

JOURNAL
how customers discover brand

AUDIO: **brand podcast**

VISUAL: **brand shows & live streams**

WRITE ARTICLES: **online & print media**

PRESS: **publicity plan & interviews**

COLLABORATIONS: **brands & influencers**

ADVERTISING: **types & placements**

MARKETING: **digital collateral**

MARKETING: **traditional collateral**

mission statement

daily goals

weekly goals

three month goals

one year goals

five year goals

ten year goals

JOURNAL

how's it going?

physically

intellectually

financially

socially

professionally

spiritually

relaxation levels

living space

LIST
expert skills

- ●
- ●
- ●
- ●
- ●

LIST
unique qualities

- ●
- ●
- ●
- ●
- ●

LIST
brand value to customers

- ●
- ●
- ●
- ●
- ●

LIST
achievements

- ●
- ●
- ●
- ●
- ●

LIST
vulnerabilities

- ●
- ●
- ●
- ●
- ●

revenue streams	problem solved	value created

operating expenses	sales goals	profits
•	•	•
•	•	•
•	•	•
•	•	•
•	•	•
total	total	total

CHECKLIST
customer communication

- [ ] website
- [ ] email
- [ ] text
- [ ] phone call
- [ ] direct messages
- [ ] _____

PRESS RELEASE
outlets press release sent to:

LIST
how people describe me
- •
- •
- •
- •
- •

LIST
customer opinions
- •
- •
- •
- •
- •

LIST
events for customers
- •
- •
- •
- •
- •

LIST
things to learn
- •
- •
- •
- •
- •

LIST
inspirational brands
- •
- •
- •
- •
- •

LIST
favorite books & shows
- •
- •
- •
- •
- •

JOURNAL
how customers discover brand

AUDIO: **brand podcast**

VISUAL: **brand shows & live streams**

WRITE ARTICLES: **online & print media**

PRESS: **publicity plan & interviews**

COLLABORATIONS: **brands & influencers**

ADVERTISING: **types & placements**

MARKETING: **digital collateral**

MARKETING: **traditional collateral**

thank you

CPSIA information can be obtained
at www.ICGtesting.com
Printed in the USA
BVHW012031271220
596502BV00011B/84